Dancing on the Graves of Your Past

Experience the Journey
Companion Workbook

Yvonne Martinez

Dancing on the Graves of Your Past Workbook

Dancing on the Graves of Your Past Workbook
Copyright © 2009 by Yvonne Martinez

All rights reserved

This book is protected by the copyright law of the United States of America.

This book may not be copied or reprinted for commercial gain or profit.

Unless otherwise noted, all Scripture quotations are from

the Holy Bible,
New International Version. Copyright © 1973, 1978, 1984,
International Bible Society. Used by permission of Zondervan.

All rights reserved.

The "NIV" and "New International Version" trademarks are registered in the United States Patent and Trademark Office by International Bible Society. Use of either trademark requires the permission of International Bible Society.

ISBN is 1449549411

EAN-13 is 9781449549411.

Published and Distributed by Stillwater Lavender

Printed in the United States of America

Order through

www.StillwaterLavender.com

Workbook is a companion to Yvonne's book, *Dancing on the Graves of Your Past*

A group facilitator's leadership guide is available if you would like to do this workbook in a support group setting.

"I pray also that the eyes of your heart may be enlightened in order that you may know the hope to which he has called you, the riches of his glorious inheritance in the saints, and his incomparably great power for us who believe."
— Eph. 1: 18

Dancing on the Graves of Your Past Workbook

Table of Contents

Chapter 1   The Past   5

Chapter 2   The Invitation   13

Chapter 3   Old Music   25

Chapter 4   Old Dances   41

Chapter 5   Dance of Surrender   49

Chapter 6   Dance of Forgiveness   63

Chapter 7   Dance of the Overcomer   83

Chapter 8   Dance of the Kingdom   99

Chapter 9   Dance Face to Face   105

Yesteryears

Sad, cruel memories

of life's dark path

rehearse in your mind.

The clouds engulf you

thundering the pain

of yesterday's great fears.

Trust the Savior

living inside you

to blow away the storm.

Pick up your banner

shout new praises

the victory has been won.

The foe already

lost the war

through Calvary's crimson flow.

Don't let tears

from yesteryears

wash the Son from your life today.

Don't let the tears

from yesteryears

wash away today.

—Yvonne Martinez

"In the plan of the Great Dance plans without number interlock, and each movement becomes in its season the breaking into flower of the whole design to which all else had been directed. Thus each is equally at the centre and none are there by being equals, but some by giving place and some by receiving it, the small things by their smallness and the great by their greatness, and all the patterns linked and looped together by the unions of a kneeling with a sceptred love. Blessed be He!"
C.S. Lewis, Perelandra, excerpt from pp. 218-219

Chapter 1

The Past

"He brought them out of darkness and the deepest gloom and broke away their chains."
—Psalm 107:14

Read *Dancing on the Graves of Your Past*, Chapter 1 ~

Paul, in Romans 8:38-39, writes, "For I am convinced that neither death nor life, neither angels nor demons, neither the present nor the future, nor any powers, neither height nor depth, nor anything else in all creation, will be able to separate us from the love of God that is in Christ Jesus our Lord." Paul mentions the present and the future, but he doesn't mention the past. The past can't separate you from God's love because He sent Jesus, His love incarnate, to redeem the past. But the past can separate you from the awareness of God's love.

What is your story?

Dancing o the Graves of Your Past Workbook

Dancing on the Graves of Your Past Workbook

God partnered with us in our past when He gave us Jesus who died on the Cross and shed His Blood. Jesus took our sins and spiritual death upon Himself and through a Divine exchange, gave us complete amnesty and freedom.

When we accept Jesus' death in exchange for ours, His Cross becomes the grave site where our sin (including mistakes and bad choices) and old nature are atoned for, dead and buried, never more to be counted against us.

Then Jesus resurrected from the dead and returned to His Father in Heaven creating a bridge of reconciliation uniting Heaven and earth. Jesus now becomes the model we follow. He was a man in right relationship with God. We now have both the authority and power to be "the sons of God"… and daughters, too!

Seated with Him in Heavenly places with full access to the Kingdom's benefits, we have freedom from emotional distress, physical sickness, and spiritual torment.

God partnered with us in our past so we could now partner with Him in our future. God did it for love. He did it to destroy the works of the devil. He did it so we would be reconciled to Him. He did it so we would have a future and a hope.

If you have accepted God's gift of Jesus, it means you have accepted Jesus death on the Cross as redemption for all your sins and mistakes. It also means you have been given eternity in Heaven AND life abundant here on Earth.

Write out your experience of accepting Jesus as Savior.

Dancing o the Graves of Your Past Workbook

Write out your experience with receiving the infilling of the Holy Spirit?

Chapter 2

The Invitation

"But for you who revere my name, the sun of righteousness
will rise with healing in its wings. And you will go out
and leap like calves released from the stall.
Then you will trample down the wicked; they will be
ashes under the soles of your feet..."
—Malachi 4:2-3

Read *Dancing on the Graves of Your Past*, Chapter 2 ~

In *My Utmost for His Highest*, Oswald Chambers says that our knowing Him is like a man coming out of a dark cave into the brightness of His light. At first we can't see well, maybe even blinded by the brightness of the light, until our eyes get adjusted and we can see clearly.

He is waiting to show you the mysteries of the Kingdom, just as He did with His disciples. God's availability isn't the barrier. The barrier is our misconception or mistrust of Him. Barriers are dissolved when we catch the revelation of who He is. What creates a victim is not what has happens to us, but remaining stuck in a pattern of thinking, believing there are limited, or no, choices.

A "victim mentality" places a ceiling on options and choices. We actually exchange the truth for a lie, and stay trapped in a cycle of unsuccessful attempts to fix something broken using broken tools.

Israel made a mistake in believing the Lord had led them into despair. They asked, "Why is the Lord bringing us to this land only to let us fall by the sword?" (Num. 14:3). Over and over they thought that bad circumstances amounted to fatal situations.

Peter, after Jesus' crucifixion, was confronted about his association with Jesus and lied (Matt. 26:69,70). In the midst of confusion and uncertainty Peter couldn't hang onto what he had known to be true about Jesus or Jesus' teachings. Overcome by fear and doubt, Peter moved into unbelief based on his circumstances.

After Jesus' burial in the tomb Mary's heart was broken believing Jesus was gone. Grief stricken over Jesus' death, she was weeping at the tomb's entrance. Mary, focused on her grief, was unaware Jesus was behind her until He called her by name (John 20:15).

These examples teach us three valuable principles.

- As long as we can trust the Lord and wait on Him, there is opportunity to see His ability to rescue and redeem us.
- Losing the ability to make choices removes hope.
- Choosing a desperate course of action often results in unfortunate experiences.

In what ways are you impatient or mistrusting that God can take care of you?

In what ways do you try to control your own destiny?

So, how's that working for you?

Until we learn differently, we can make the mistake of believing God is like a person we know—someone who failed to love, nourish, or accept; or someone who failed to love enough to correct and confront.

God's desire for you is greater then you can imagine or think. "…no mind has conceived what God has prepared for those who love Him" (1Cor.2:9). God has prepared things for us that are beyond our imagination and exceed our mental capacity. Our minds are a great creation of God, but our mind can hinder and limit our receptivity to experience the greatness of the Kingdom. We were meant to be ruled by our spirit, in-filled with His Holy Spirit. Filled with unbelief, doubt and fear, we journey through the maze of our minds to find answers, rather than into His Presence.

Jesus said if I was born again, I would be able to see the Kingdom (John 3:3). Jesus is talking about a revelatory experience here and now. The Kingdom is available to us, but we have to put on our "son" glasses to access it. God wants you to have full access to the benefits Jesus died for—that includes you getting your full Kingdom inheritance, the "life more abundantly" talked about in John 10:10.

My pastor, Bill Johnson, says what you think you know will hold you back from what you need to know unless you remain a novice. The biggest challenge we face is to remain open to "all things are possible with God" (Matt: 19:26).

Read the first chapter of Ephesians. This chapter is full of God's blessings to us who believe and a reminder of what a heritage we have in Jesus. What does it tell you?

Which declarations, provisions and promises in Ephesians 1 are you embracing and living in partnership with? Don't write "the right answers" or what you have been taught to be true. Be honest and let your heart speak to you.

_____
_____
_____
_____
_____
_____
_____
_____
_____
_____
_____
_____
_____
_____
_____
_____
_____
_____
_____

Which declarations provisions and promises in this same chapter are challenging for you to embrace or believe? Don't write "the right answers" or what you have been taught to be true. Be honest and let your heart speak to you.

_____
_____
_____
_____
_____
_____
_____
_____
_____
_____
_____
_____
_____
_____
_____
_____
_____
_____
_____

This next exercise is to help you take a closer look at a particular past issue.

- **First, reread your story from Chapter 1.**

- **Then pray...** *"Papa God...You know all the details of my life. Which event do you want to bring to my attention right now?"*

The prayer is asking Him to search your heart. In other words, you are asking Papa God from the story you wrote, which ones He wants to bring to the front to work on right now.

- **As soon as you finish the prayer, you will listen and then write out the first things He brings up. It may be something obvious or it may be something different that you originally overlooked.**

Ready...

Now pray, *"Papa God, You know all the details of my life. Which event do You want to bring to my attention right now?"* Write the first thing He shows you.

1. _____
   _____

Now again, *"Papa God, is there another event You want to bring to my attention right now?"* Write the first thing He shows you.

2. _____

Now again, *"Papa God, is there another event You want to bring to my attention right now?"* Write the first thing He shows you.

3. _____

Continue until you feel that is all there is for now.

4. _____

5. _____

6. _____

Look over the list you just accumulated and ask Papa to highlight just one situation to use through out the balance of the workbook. This will establish a format for you to use in the future. With that event in mind, answer the following questions.

- **How old were you at the time this occurred?**

    My example… "I was 9 years old"

    _____

- **What happened?**

    My example… "I witnessed my dad attack and attempt to rape my mom. My mom called for me to help and when I came into the room I saw my dad hitting my mom and attempt to rape her. He pulled at her clothes and was yelling at her. He was naked. When he saw me, he grabbed me and pushed me out of the room and I hit my head against the door. My mom screamed and I couldn't help. I don't remember how we got out of the house but I never saw my dad again for a long time.

    _____
    _____
    _____
    _____
    _____
    _____

- **What was your response to what happened?**

    My example…"I mostly felt afraid and worried if my dad would try to find out where we were. I thought he might break into our house and hurt us again. I didn't feel safe. When I went to school I felts ashamed about what had happened. I kept it all a secret and lied telling others that my dad died. I was glad we were away from him because I was afraid of him and didn't feel safe around him."

Dancing on the Graves of Your Past Workbook

Chapter 3

Old Music

"The dead man came out, his hands and feet wrapped with strips of linen, and a cloth around his face. Jesus said to them, Take off the grave clothes and let him go."

—John 11:44

Read *Dancing on the Graves of Your Past*, Chapter 3 ~

Most of us are born with the belief we are safe. However, when abuse occurs, trust and safety is breached. Intrusion through trust and safety can be a traumatic emotional disturbance and continued emotional disruption. Trauma is often experienced as a forced exposure interrupting and penetrating a safe environment.

Transfer the information from the event you just identified and shorten the descriptions so they are brief and more concise or direct….

#1 Write a brief description of what happened.

My brief example of what happened…"I witnessed m dad's violent attack against my mom.

#2 Write a brief description of how you responded.

My brief example of how I responded…"I was afraid, didn't feel safe and I lied."

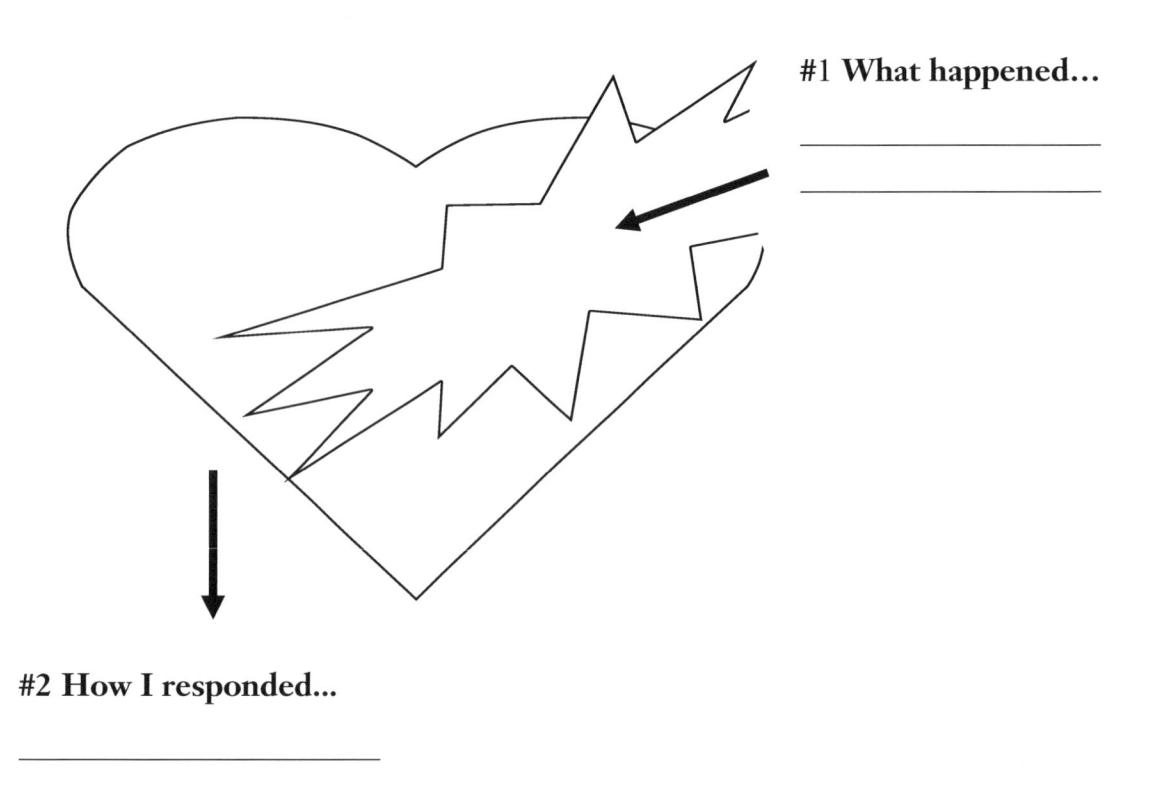

#1 What happened…

_____

_____

#2 How I responded…

_____

_____

_____

Like the music playing in the background during a movie, the memories experienced with trauma and associated feelings create a backdrop from which life is lived and choices are made. The Old Music is the trumpeting of residual pain.

Post traumatic reactions may include anxiety, terror, guilt, blaming, detachment, agitation or irritability, restlessness, loss of interest in usual activities, loss of emotional control, grief, depression, uncertainty, thoughts of suicide, withdrawal from family or friends, communication changes, "startle" reflex, sleep disturbance, change in sexual interest or function, inability to be alone, self-harm, mistrust of environment or people, changes in appetite, and sometimes obsessive, compulsive or addictive behavior.

Pray and ask Papa God to show you if there are left over symptoms from the painful event you identified in the last diagram. If He shows you something, use the arrows to describe the residual symptoms. Write down as many as He shows you.

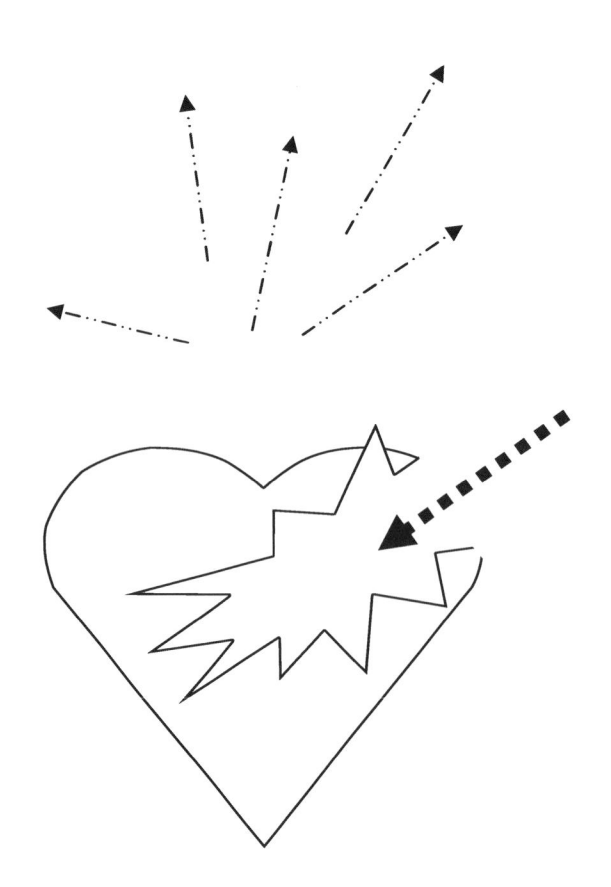

The relationship dance with the symptoms enhances the survivor's ability to stay connected with the past, allowing the memory to remain alive.

Rehearsing and replaying the music are attempts to try to understand:
- **Did it really happen?**
- **Why did it happen?**
- **How could I have stopped it?**
- **Could I have done something different?**
- **How can I get even with my abuser?**

Which of these do you relate to? _____

Keeping alive the memory of the trauma allows the person to re-enter the scenario in an attempt to find resolve. It helps people who are hurting to prove the validity of what happened. The victim is often the only witness of the trauma who can testify to the trauma's reality. The symptoms are proof, to themselves and others, the trauma was real. They feel that without displaying their symptoms they won't be believed.

With the Old Music playing in the background, we dance the dance of guilt and shame, fear and blame, rehearsing the steps we know so well. We exchange the truth for a lie, submitting to the lie, allowing it to dominate and control us. The power of the Old Music is protected by our agreement and permission for it to remain in tact. The dance with the past is both unholy and ungodly.

Abuse is the exploitation or neglect of basic human needs. It can be defined as wrongful, unreasonable, or harmful treatment by word or deed. A child who is trapped in an abusive situation is like a prisoner of war with no power, no leverage, and no voice. Abuse has many faces.

Here is a list of basic human needs:

- Survival (food, shelter, clothing)
- Safety (physical, emotional)
- Touching, skin contact
- Attention
- Mirroring and echoing
- Guidance
- Listening
- Participating
- Acceptance
- Opportunity to grieve losses and to grow
- Support
- Loyalty and trust
- Accomplishment
- Sexuality
- Enjoyment or fun
- Freedom
- Nurturing
- Unconditional love, including connection with God

Identify the needs you felt deprived of by placing a check next to the unmet need. How many needs were unmet? _____

Regarding misconceptions about abuse...

Abuse Should Be Minimized

"I guess I should be grateful it wasn't worse. This has happened to lots of people."

Have you minimized what happened to you?

_____
_____
_____

Abuse Heals with Time

"It has been five years. Why should I have to go through this again? I don't want to discuss it."

Have you felt time or distance from the pain is healing?

_____
_____
_____

Abuse Can Be Defined by the Act

"He never actually touched me, but I hated the way he looked at my body. I feel so stupid because I can't describe what he did."

Do you have a difficult time putting words to what happened?

_____
_____
_____

Why do the actions from who hurt you hold so much power over you? The Old Music has the ability to make us feel guilt or shame for what someone else did to us. I know it sounds silly, that someone would hurt you and you feel it is your fault. But it is possible to assume responsibility for the behaviors of others thereby agreeing with statements like, "It must have been my fault." Believing it was your fault is a type of false power—that you had the power to make someone behave a certain way.

You may discover that you are holding yourself responsible for the actions of others. Assuming responsibility for the sins of others can cause, what I call, "false guilt." No matter how hard you try, you cannot get rid of the guilt through repentance for these sins. They aren't yours.

Are you experiencing unresolved shame and guilt about what happened to you? Pray and ask Papa God if you have any responsibility or contribution toward your painful situation. Honesty with yourself is essential. Our agreement with the lie that it is, or was, our responsibility or our fault keeps the memory empowered. What you believe to be true will expose the stronghold empowering the Old Music. Write what He shows you.

"Papa God, show me if there is any part of this event that I am responsible for?"

_____
_____
_____
_____
_____
_____
_____

Now ask Papa God, *"Show me which events I am NOT responsible for?"*

"Papa who is responsible? Why are they responsible?"

Write their name and what they are responsible for.

_____
_____
_____
_____
_____
_____
_____
_____

Secrets are sickness but openness is wholeness. Keeping a secret is very powerful. As long as the secret stays hidden, you hold onto a false sense of power that keeps you in control.

Have you been keeping any secrets? _____

Who are you protecting? _____

Write down what the Lord might be showing you about keeping secrets…

_____
_____
_____
_____
_____
_____

Confrontation is about courage and love and the willingness to discuss conflict. But it should be done from a place of strength. Unless the offender recognizes and accepts his or her responsibility, you will set yourself up for more rejection and hurt. If you are still in danger of being hurt, you should refrain from that relationship until you and, hopefully, the offender can get some help.

Do you feel the need to confront the person who hurt you?
_____

If so, what will you say or do?
_____
_____

One way to engage safe confrontation is to write a letter to the person being as honest as possible. The writing exercise allows you the opportunity to express how you really feel without the vulnerability of an in-person meeting.

Another way is to write a "not-to-be-mailed" letter. This exercise helps you keep a safe distance from the person. It helps you confront what happened rather than the person directly, especially if the person has passed away, the letter can be to the Lord on their behalf.

Now, you are invited and encouraged to write each responsible person a "not-to-be-mailed" letter. Remember that a not-to-be-mailed letter is *not to be mailed!* The letter doesn't have to be proper, punctuated, or perfect. This is an exercise in acknowledgment of the truth and isn't meant to be judged or corrected.

Use the following format as a guideline, duplicating it for as many letters as you feel you need to write.

To _____   or   *To Papa, on behalf of* _____

This is what you did…
_____
_____
_____
_____

You hurt me when you…
_____
_____
_____
_____

This is how it made me feel…
_____
_____
_____
_____

You are responsible for…
_____
_____
_____
_____

Your Name _____   *Date* _____

Prayer

For each letter, read it out loud then break the lie that you were responsible and ask God to show you the truth. Sample prayer...

"Papa God, I acknowledge my pain and loss and bring it before You. I ask You to forgive me for believing the lie I was responsible for what happened. I give responsibility back to the one who IS responsible. I come out of agreement with carrying the sin of someone else and blaming myself for their actions and wrong doing. I break the lie that I am responsible and come out of agreement with false guilt or shame. Papa, would You show me the truth?"

Write down what He shows you.

_____
_____
_____
_____
_____
_____
_____
_____
_____
_____
_____
_____
_____
_____
_____
_____
_____
_____
_____
_____

Before closing, wait and listen for anything you feel God may be saying to you.

You can be assured what you feel or hear is from God when it lines up with what the Bible says. His impressions, songs, psalms, and words can bring true peace. This peace isn't an absence of conflict but the inner assurance that God cares for you.

Write down anything you hear from Papa God right now.

_____
_____
_____
_____
_____
_____
_____
_____
_____
_____
_____
_____
_____
_____
_____
_____
_____

Ask Papa God what to do with the "not-to-be-mailed" letter you wrote… What did He tell you?

_____

Chapter 4

Old Dances

"Surely you desire truth in the inner parts; you teach me wisdom in the inmost place. Cleanse me with hyssop, and I will be clean; wash me, and I will be whiter than snow. Let me hear joy and gladness; let the bones you have crushed rejoice. Hide your face from my sins and blot out all my iniquity. Create in me a pure heart, O God, and renew a steadfast spirit within me. Do not cast me from your presence or take your Holy Spirit from me. Restore to me the joy of your salvation and grant me a willing spirit, to sustain me. "

—Psalm 51:6-12

Read *Dancing on the Graves of Your Past*, Chapter 4 ~

The Old Dances are the coping mechanisms we use to cover the shame and guilt from our actions and choices. The Old Dances of guilt and shame are sustained by the lyrics, melodies, and chorus changes (Old Music) we knew by heart. The Old Dance chooses distance rather than relationship. Distance (fear and hiding) enables us to remain in control.

Conflict is created when what we believe doesn't match up to what God tells us in His Word.

- I believe (God and my feelings/experiences agree)
- I want to believe (God and my feelings/experiences conflict)
- I don't believe (My feelings/experiences outweigh what He says)

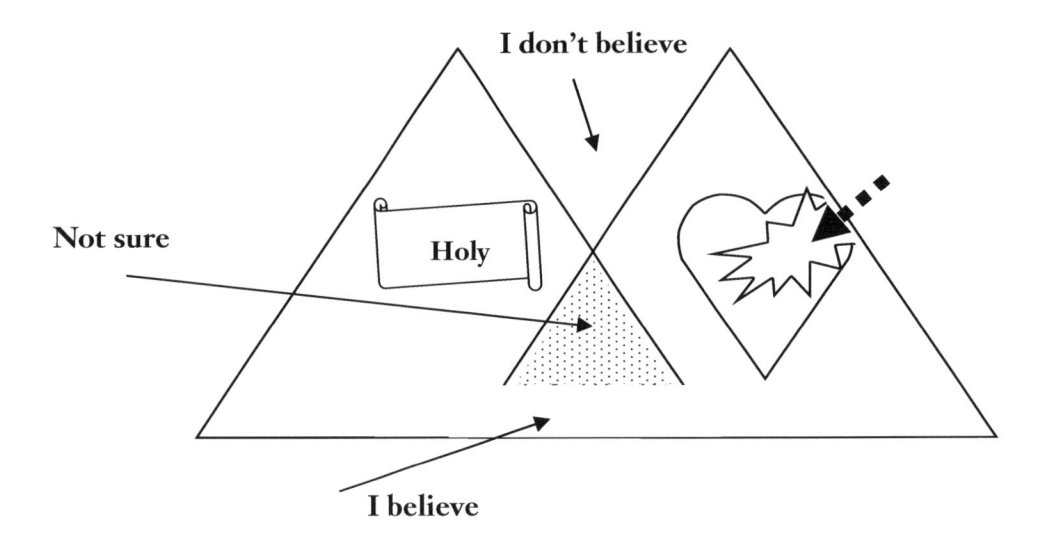

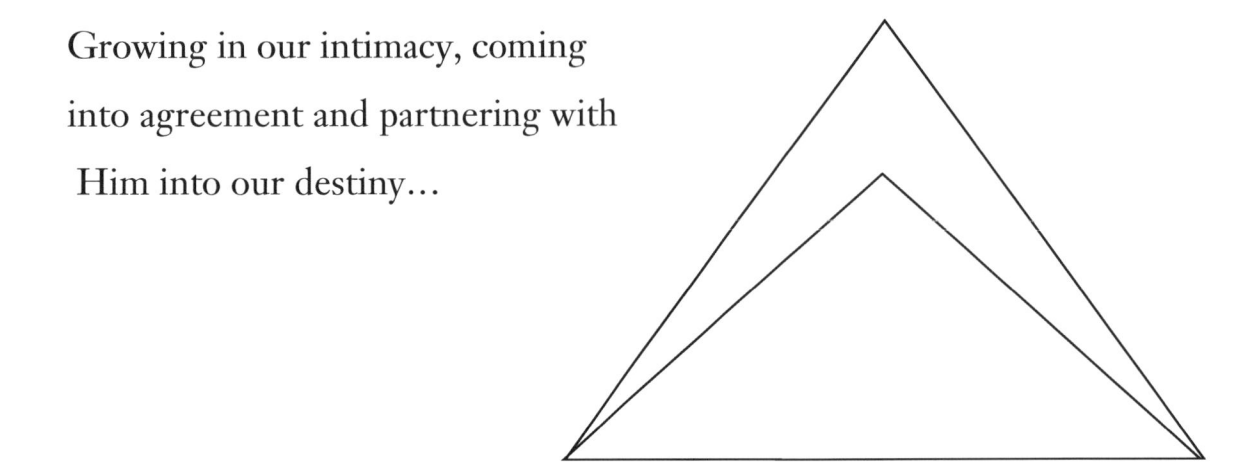

Growing in our intimacy, coming into agreement and partnering with Him into our destiny…

The more uncomfortable process of the Holy Spirit reveals our connection to the Old Dances, our hurtful actions and attitudes toward others. It is God's answer to our prayer from Psalm 51:6-12 to "create in me a pure heart."

Look up Psalm 51 and read verses 6-12.

As children, we often needed self-protection to survive deprivation, neglect, or violence. As adults, our learned ways of protection can become the walls that close us in and keep everyone else out. Walls of self-protection become the obstacles that block intimate relationships.

Self-protective patterns can become the broken glasses through which life is viewed. Adults living with residual pain (Old Music) and recurring coping patterns (Old Dances) become imprisoned. The patterns that once protected now keep us locked up and the adult heart flutters and fights against the bars for freedom, thus the dances are in full swing.

Adults who live their lives through a coping mechanism or from a defensive position repeat patterns in choices and select, by default, the same unfulfilling reactions. They choose and make future decisions based on underlying false beliefs. The coping behavior is a vehicle to keep the pain shielded, like a bandage covering an open wound.

Walls are often reinforced with self-pity. Self-pity strategically accesses guilt and shame through the pain of the Old Music.

Feelings of rejection, betrayal, hatred, anger, unforgiveness, and ambivalence are natural responses to being hurt. But when we harbor and protect them, we often reshape them into weapons to hurt ourselves or others.

The coping mechanism or protective attitude reveals itself through sinful behaviors, manipulation and compromised actions.

Ask the Lord to show you coping mechanisms you employ to keep yourself protected or to avoid dealing with painful issues.

1. _____
2. _____
3. _____

In contrast there can be a sense of entitlement. Since all these bad things happened to me…I am entitled to compensation, free counseling, unending attention from others. I am entitled to mistreat others, be angry, and take out my pain on you.

God instructs us not to partner with darkness rather to let darkness be exposed (Eph 5:11). It is His love for us that drags what is in darkness into the light. Healing requires we remain humble and honest and allow the deep work when the Holy Spirit draws our attention to the underlying issues and the ways we have created unholy and ungodly bonding.

How has your behavior hurt others?

_____
_____
_____
_____
_____
_____
_____
_____
_____
_____
_____
_____
_____
_____
_____
_____

In what way do you justify or excuse your behavior toward others?

_____
_____
_____

Dancing on the Graves of Your Past Workbook

Sinful cycles pass down from generation to generation. Look up and read Exodus 34:7 and Numbers 14:18. Ask Papa God to show you which behaviors are generational and "learned" from your family or environment.

"Papa God, what behaviors do I demonstrate that are like my mother or her side of the family?"

_____
_____
_____
_____
_____
_____
_____
_____

"Papa God, what behaviors do I demonstrate that are like my father or his side of the family?"

_____
_____
_____
_____
_____
_____
_____
_____

According to 2 Cor. 5:21, "God made him who had no sin to be sin for us, so that in him we might become the righteousness of God." And Psalm 112:2 gives us a promise that the generations of the upright—the righteous—will be blessed!

Read Psalm 112:2 and pronounce a written blessing on your future generations.

_____
_____
_____
_____
_____
_____
_____
_____
_____

Chapter 5

Dance of Surrender

*I will both lie down in peace, and sleep, for
you alone, O LORD, make me dwell in safety.*
— Psalm 4:8

Read *Dancing on the Graves of Your Past*, Chapter 5 ~

Jesus danced the Dance of Surrender so He and His Father would be "One." It was the beginning of Jesus following His Father's direction so in all ways He would be submitted to His Father. The Dance of Surrender is coming out of yourself and into God. It is about trusting Him—allowing Him to lead us into true freedom and peace.

Giving our problems to Jesus requires an emptying of self-will and self-protection. The "coming" must be accompanied with sincere motivation and desire to be rid of our "yuck." Resistance to surrender will drive us to the edge and limit of our own strength.

What does the Old Music and Old Dance offer that generates resistance to surrender? The answers are in the completion of the following statement. Circle the statements that best represent your resistance.

If I keep this trauma-bond relationship in tact I won't have to...

feel, have an identity, face others, be responsible, be authentic, change, tell secrets, be honest, tell my truth, trust, be in reality, be positive, grow, be accountable, have relationships, be mature, risk, have goals, have values, be independent, have freedom, have internal validation, have a purpose, be connected with people or family, have dreams, have hopes, be successful, have faith, live, be in the present, obtain status, make decisions, have needs, have wants, have communication, intimacy with God or...

_____

_____

Surrender can expose and trigger pain of vulnerability as that which we first experienced during the original trauma. Remember, when I was talking about trauma being a forced intrusion into a safe environment? The person in protective mode perceives themselves as now being safe. Protection is a disguise. Any intrusion into that artificially safe place is felt as penetrating and painful.

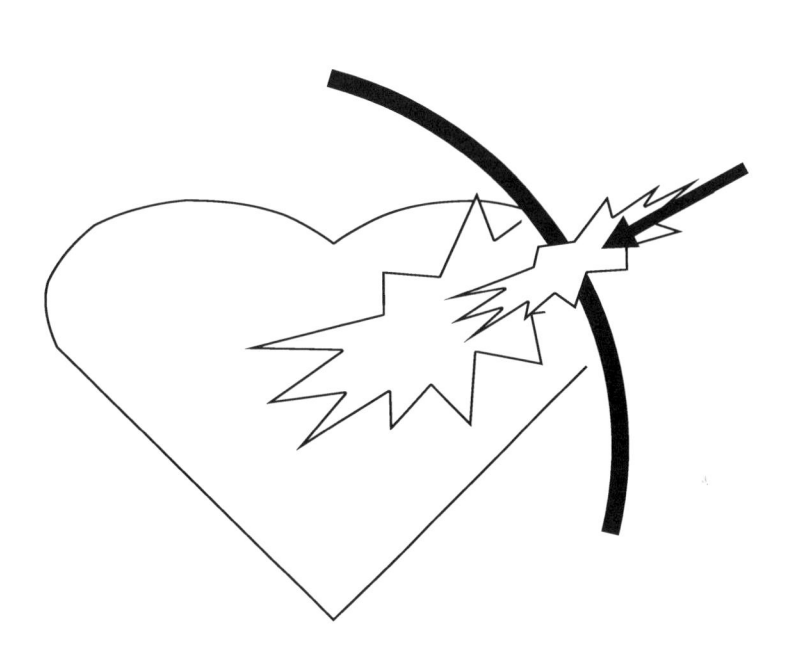

Define an intrusion into your presumed safe place.

_____
_____
_____

Resistance to intimacy is fortified by our protective barriers. The barriers are fortified by the promises we made to the Old Music and Old Dances.

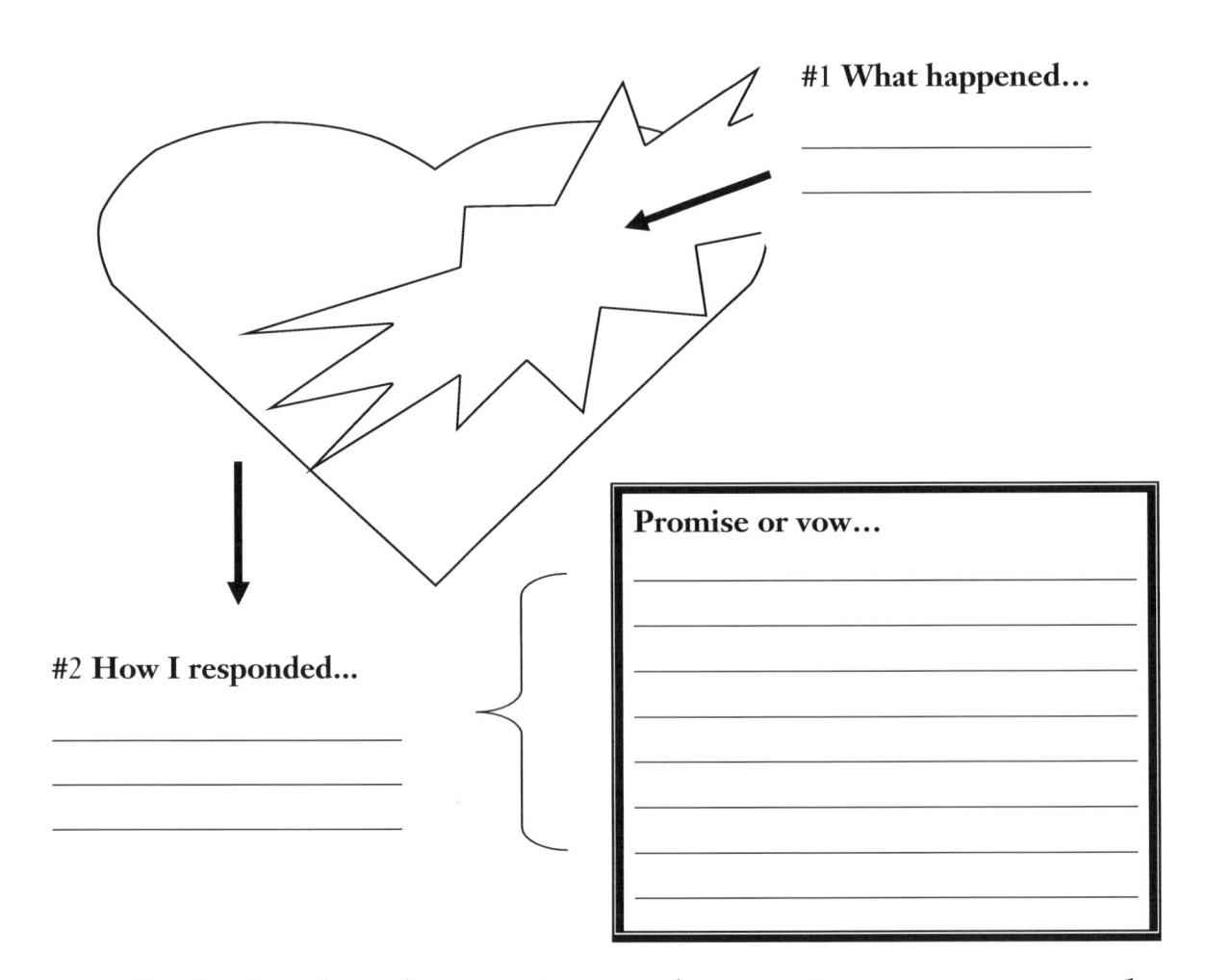

#1 What happened…

#2 How I responded…

Promise or vow…

In the bracket above, write out the promise or vow you made as a result of what happened and your response.

My example…"I made a vow that I didn't need anyone to love me because love hurt.

Read John, Chapter 14

Jesus tells Thomas and the disciples "I will not leave you as orphans...." Jesus discerned Thomas' insecurity and fear.

Jesus identifies an "orphan" spirit manifested in Thomas' fear of being left alone, unprotected, uncovered, rejected and abandoned.

The orphan spirit is drawn through the lack of protection and covering. It only has access because there was an unmet need, a place of trauma and a place of vulnerability. Triggering the pain of vulnerability and the absence of covering, the orphan spirit opens the door to other protectors.

In what way do you identify with an orphan spirit?

Three prominent protectors willingly join the orphan spirit. They are the unloving spirit, the religious spirit and the punishing spirit. If these barriers exist, they must be conquered so surrender will be pure and unhindered, or manipulated.

The Unloving Spirit

The unloving spirit protects the orphaned heart by blocking the ability to give and receive love both from others and God. Its melody plays in harmony with the Old Music, rooted in the past and its footsteps can be tracked throughout the Old Dances. Out of default, the unloving spirit will reject before it gets rejected—it will desire love but behave unlovely.

Love actually brings justice and requires protection. Those who are unable to give and receive love reject the work of the Cross and the Blood of Jesus and thereby reject the "love" God sent them.

The unloving spirit manipulates the orphan heart with unworthiness, pity, condemnation, and justification. It judges, accuses, criticizes and manipulates. It will embrace the comfortably uncomfortable, rather than surrender to God's love.

In what way do you identify with an unloving spirit?

_____
_____
_____
_____
_____
_____
_____
_____
_____
_____
_____
_____
_____
_____
_____
_____
_____

The Religious Spirit

The religious spirit covers the orphaned heart with performance and works. Completing a fifteen-week self-defense course, their lives in neat little packages, and along comes the "invitation" to give it all up! "You must be kidding! I have worked very hard to get where I am and no one is going to take it from me again. Only the strong survive."

The orphaned heart's pain is covered by masks of overeating, oversleeping, overworking, or addictions to pornography, alcohol, drugs, or self-injury. Sometimes the religious spirit is manifested in fear, hiding the orphan heart behind locks, security buildings, police dogs, whistles, or self-defense classes; maybe hiding behind anger, verbal abuse, assault, pride, procrastination and even apathy or hopelessness.

Consequently, the religious spirit is fixated on self-reliance and those things which they can control. Within the Old Music and Old Dance they have created a fortress and any uninvited intrusion reinforces the barriers.

Principles that hold higher value than relationship create form without purpose and tradition without power. The religious spirit is self-imposed control.

In what way do you identify with a religious spirit?

_____
_____
_____
_____
_____
_____
_____
_____

Punishing Spirit

The punishing spirit denies the work of the Cross, the Blood of Jesus and the Resurrection as full and complete payment for our sin and mistakes. It blocks receiving amnesty and forgiveness demanding greater payment. wer. Continuing to punish ourselves for the reasons Christ died for us leads to self-destruction.

The punishing spirit strikes with a whip entitled "regret," strategically mutilating hope, confidence and encouragement. It rises in contest to the power of Jesus' Blood.

The punishing spirit gateways to "hope deferred that makes the heart sick" (Prov.13:12) rather than hope in the finished work of the Cross (Heb. 6:19). It will cause you to feel unworthy of receiving God's healing power.

In what way do you identify with a punishing spirit?

_____
_____
_____
_____
_____
_____
_____
_____
_____
_____
_____
_____
_____

The antidote for the orphan spirit and it's allies is experiencing the Holy Spirit. The Holy Spirit, counselor and comforter, brings the Spirit of Adoption to encircle and fill the wounded heart, drawing us into the "Papa, Daddy" relationship so desperately needed.

"For you did not receive a spirit that makes you a slave again to fear, but you have received the Spirit of Sonship. And by him we cry, Abba Father. The Spirit himself testifies with our spirit that we are God's children." (Romans 8:15,16)

Would you like to receive the Spirit of Adoption?

_____
_____

Ask Papa to prepare your heart to receive ...

_____
_____
_____
_____
_____
_____

We cannot truly surrender with hands grasping the grave's head stone. We must surrender with hands grasping the Kingdom. Through conflict and pain we can enter the Kingdom and apprehend it.

"Awake, O sleeper, and rise from the dead, the light shine in your heart to reveal the Kingdom."

Eph. 5:14

"Taste and see that the Lord is good; blessed is the man who takes refuge in him."

Psalm 34:8,

Surrender is the loving process whereby we willingly let go of the Old Music and Old Dances while being romanced in the arms of Jesus into Kingdom reality. We let go while we hang on!

Surrender is an opportunity to deal with pain in a different way. How we deal with pain is a lesson in dealing with evil. Rather than looking for an escape it requires actually holding onto the pain long enough to take it to God.

Loss positions you for justice and transparency unleashes breakthrough. The perils and tribulations of living in a fallen world give us an opportunity to press into His Presence.

Yielding

Teach me, Jesus, how to pray

more like you, have your way.

Create the words within my heart,

so from my lips they do impart.

Teach me in the silent hour,

to wait upon your strength and power.

Mold my life like yielding clay

in your footsteps, every day.

Jesus Christ, ever so sweet,

with nail scarred hands and feet,

I bury old self with you this day

and resurrect in power, your way.

—Yvonne Martinez

Chapter 6

Dance of Forgiveness

"Give, and it will be given to you. A good measure,
pressed down, shaken together and running over,
will be poured into your lap. For with the measure you
use, it will be measured to you."
—Luke 6:38

Read *Dancing on the Graves of Your Past*, Chapter 6 ~

Surrender and forgiveness are necessary for authentic intimacy with Him. They reveal dependency, love and trust, keeping our hearts pure. Forgiveness is a fruit of surrender. In forgiving, we release our judgment or desire for revenge. Forgiveness is the courage to let mercy triumph over judgment.

Read James 2:13

What is your response to the paragraphs in <u>*Dancing on the Graves of Your Past,*</u> pages 143 – 149?

Giving forgiveness to those who hurt us

_____
_____
_____
_____

Giving forgiveness to those who are not sorry

_____
_____
_____
_____

Giving forgiveness when you don't feel like it

_____
_____
_____
_____

Giving forgiveness to those who persist in abusing you

_____
_____
_____
_____
_____

Giving forgiveness when you are angry

_____
_____
_____
_____
_____

What is your response to the paragraphs in _Dancing on the Graves of Your Past_, pages 157 - 162?

Forgiveness isn't denying the pain

_____
_____
_____

Forgiveness isn't excusing the crime

_____
_____
_____

Forgiveness isn't reconciliation

_____
_____
_____

Forgiveness isn't reconciliation, but it is a start

_____
_____
_____

Read 1John 1:9, Psalm 103:3, and 147:3

What is God showing you about these scriptures?

_____
_____
_____
_____
_____
_____

There is a cleansing and healing element associated with God's forgiveness. The purity of Jesus' shed Blood washes us, not just covering over, but removing any stain or odor, any residue or evidence. Receiving forgiveness is partnering with God's love.

Prayer

"Papa God, I want to partner with Your love. I no longer want to hold unforgiveness in my heart. I am ready to surrender and let go of anything holding me back from receiving all You have for me."

"Papa God, who do I need to forgive?" Write down the first names of the people He shows you.

_____

_____

_____

_____

_____

For each person He reveals, use the following prayer format...

"I forgive _____ for

(listen to what the Lord shows you before you fill in the blanks)

_____

_____

_____

I confess I have carried judgment and offence. I ask forgiveness for my actions of _____."

I hand this person to You...

Do a prophetic act and actually hand off and release them to God.

After you finish forgiving those He shows you, ask…

"Papa God, now that I have forgiven, what do You have for me in exchange?"

What did He give you?

_____
_____
_____
_____
_____
_____
_____
_____

How do you feel now?

_____
_____
_____
_____
_____
_____
_____
_____

What do good boundaries look like for those relationships that are still difficult or unsafe?

*"Have mercy on me, O God, according to your unfailing love;
according to your great compassion blot out my transgressions.
Wash away all my iniquity and cleanse me from my sin."*
Ps. 51:1, 2

For each of your own protective actions or behavior attitudes, ask Papa to forgive you for any way you trusted in the protector and didn't trust Him.

"Papa God, You have known my heart all along and never stopped loving me, even when I wasn't able to trust You. Thank You for showing me how the protective behavior/attitude of

_____

*has kept me from being closer to You.
Please forgive me for*

_____,

setting me free from guilt and shame, according to Your Word.

I come out of agreement with the need for this protector/behavior and renounce the ungodly or unholy alliance. I hand

_____

to You and tell it bye-bye...so long!"

Is there anything you would like to add to your prayer?

_____
_____
_____

Now ask Him, *"Papa God, do You forgive me?"*

What did He say?

_____
_____
_____

Do you accept Papa God's forgiveness?

_____
_____
_____

If so, then write it out... *"Yes, Papa God, I accept Your forgiveness, mercy, and love."*

_____
_____

Now ask, *"Papa God, what do You have for me in exchange?"*

_____
_____
_____
_____

Is there anything you want to add to your prayer?

_____
_____
_____

Write anything additional Papa is showing you…

_____
_____
_____
_____
_____

For any way you have hurt others because of your protective actions or behavior attitudes, ask Papa to forgive you.

"Papa God, You have known my heart all along and never stopped loving me, even when I took out my pain on others. Thank You for showing me how the protective behavior/attitude of

_____

has hurt others and created barriers in personal relationships. Please forgive me for

_____,

setting me free from guilt and shame, according to Your Word.

I come out of agreement with the need to blame or shame others through this protector/behavior and renounce the ungodly or unholy alliance.

I hand

_____

to You and tell it bye-bye…so long!"

Is there anything you would like to add to your prayer?

_____
_____
_____

Now ask Him, *"Papa God, do You forgive me?"*

What did He say?

_____
_____
_____

Do you accept Papa God's forgiveness?

_____
_____

If so, then write it out… " *Yes, Papa God, I accept Your forgiveness, mercy, and love.*"

_____
_____

Now ask, *"Papa God, what do You have for me in exchange?"*

_____
_____
_____
_____

Is there anything you want to add to your prayer?

_____
_____
_____

Write anything additional Papa is showing you...

_____
_____
_____
_____
_____

Secrets and False Power...

"Papa, I ask You to forgive me for carrying secrets or for believing I have the power to cause people to behave in a certain way, both are types of false power. I come out of agreement with the belief that I have supernatural power outside of You.

I renounce saying anything "was my fault" if it wasn't my fault and come out of agreement with any form of witchcraft that would have led me to believe I have power over anyone."

What is Papa showing you now?

_____
_____
_____
_____
_____

Forgiving yourself is sometimes the most difficult. Ask Papa God… *"Am I holding anything against myself?"* **Write what He shows you.**

_____
_____
_____
_____
_____
_____
_____
_____
_____

"Papa, God, what do I need to forgive myself for?"

_____
_____
_____
_____
_____

Ask Papa God to give you a picture of yourself at the time of the event (you identified this age when you first recorded the event). You will use this picture as a focal point for prayer. After God gives you a picture of yourself, hold onto that image and answer the following…

How old are you in the picture? _____

How were you feeling?

_____
_____
_____
_____
_____
_____
_____
_____
_____
_____
_____

Using the image as a point of prayer...

> " *(your name)* _____, *I forgive you for*
>
> *(write as many things as Papa shows you)*

My example: Yvonne, I forgive you for being needy, for feeling lonely, for misbehaving for attention...

_____
_____
_____
_____
_____

_____
_____

And

I ask you to forgive me for judging you, being angry with you, rejecting you, shaming you, disconnecting from you, even hating you…
(finish in your own words)

_____
_____
_____
_____
_____
_____
_____
_____

When you feel ready, continue with the following

"(your name) _____, I a sorry for the things I have held against you and I am sorry for not allowing you to be cleansed and washed by Jesus Blood…I now invite you now to receive Jesus Blood to wash and cover you…(pause for His presence to meet with you) and I invite you back into my heart."

After you have finished forgiving yourself, ask Papa God what He wants to give you in exchange…write down what He gives you!

_____
_____

_____
_____
_____
_____
_____
_____
_____

How do you feel now?

_____
_____
_____
_____
_____
_____

The truth is that Jesus died for every issue in your life. You are just now receiving His Blood, His Love, His Forgiveness, and His Mercy into those areas you previously felt were unworthy of His redemption.

Wait to listen for anything additional God wants to tell you and write it down.

_____
_____
_____
_____

Breaking Soul Ties

- If there has been a dysfunctional ungodly or unholy relationship with this person such as co-dependency, people pleasing, poor boundaries, continued thinking about them or the situation, idolatry, etc…

- If there was sexual relationship, whether it was abuse or consensual, forgiving the person and breaking soul ties is important. ..

When you break soul ties you are cutting off, in the spirit, an ungodly and unholy alliance to a person or situation. Whether you were aware of this or not, these connections can establish priority and your allegiance to them creates an obstacle to freedom.

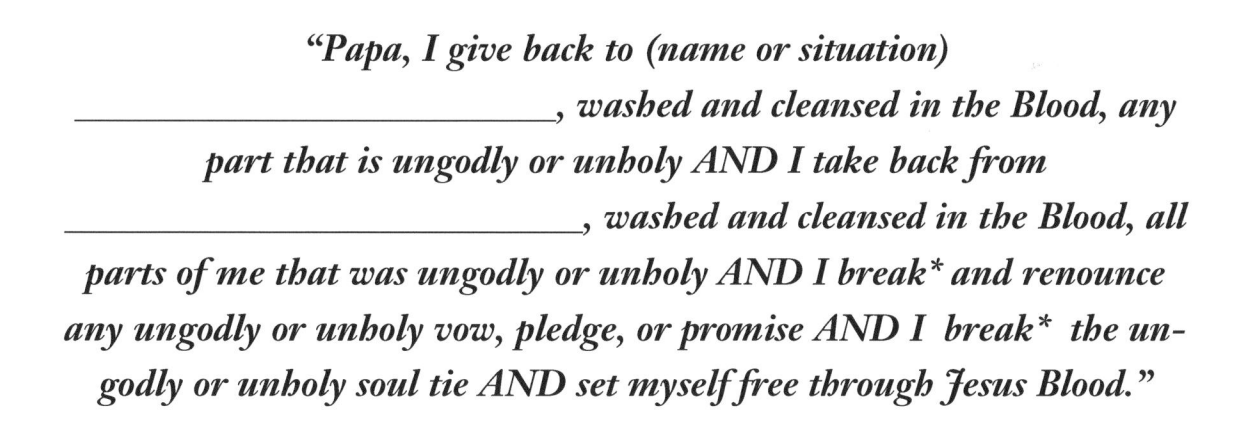

"Papa, I give back to (name or situation) _____, washed and cleansed in the Blood, any part that is ungodly or unholy AND I take back from _____, washed and cleansed in the Blood, all parts of me that was ungodly or unholy AND I break* and renounce any ungodly or unholy vow, pledge, or promise AND I break* the ungodly or unholy soul tie AND set myself free through Jesus Blood."

*NOTE: When you say the word "break", in any of the prayers, I want you to do a prophetic act and clap as loud as you can…this declaration shifts the atmosphere and makes an announcement on your behalf!

- If there are generational sins or curses…

"Papa, I stand in repentance on behalf of past generations for the sins of

_____

and ask for forgiveness on their behalf.

I come out of agreement on behalf of past generations and come out of agreement for the sins

of

_____.

AND break* the word curses

of

_____

off myself, my generation and the generations to come..

I give back to those generations (name or situation) _____, washed and cleansed in the Blood, any part that was ungodly or unholy AND I take back from those generations (name or situation) _____, washed and cleansed in the Blood, all vows, pledges, promises that were ungodly or unholy AND I break* and renounce any word curse AND I break* the ungodly or unholy soul tie AND set myself and my family free, my generation and the generations to come, through Jesus Blood."

We also need to resolve the question of anger towards God. It's often easier to forgive a person than to forgive God. After all, God is well aware of the events that happened in our life, and yet, circumstances didn't change. If we become embittered with God we will build a shell of resistance that will insulate us from His presence.

God is good. God is love. A good, loving God does not order disaster into our life to teach us a lesson. He wasn't out to lunch when bad things happened.

God doesn't send us diseases to make us better Christians. The source of affliction is our enemy who uses bad circumstances to build a case of unbelief against God. However, God will use the circumstances to draw us to Him, if we will come.

Jesus suffered and paid the price for our healing and freedom. Jesus was the remedy for God's wrath and the substitute for God's punishment. Jesus took our suffering upon Himself. Jesus died so we could live emotionally, physically, spiritually, and eternally free with full access to the benefits of a good, loving God.

Ask Papa God to forgive you for blaming Him.

_____
_____
_____
_____
_____
_____
_____

"Papa God, what is the truth?"

_____
_____
_____
_____
_____
_____
_____
_____
_____
_____
_____
_____
_____
_____
_____
_____
_____
_____
_____

The truth that sets you free will never be found through mental gymnastics or religious principles. So, don't be led through a maze, a journey inward, to find the answers to your problems.

Our minds don't contain the answers, Jesus does. The answer must be found outside of ourselves, in a journey to discover Him.

Chapter 7

Dance of the Overcomer

The Lord is faithful, and he will strengthen and
protect you from the evil one.
—2 Thessalonians 3:3

Read *Dancing on the Graves of Your Past*, Chapter 7 ~

In Song of Songs 2:9,10 the "lover" comes to the "beautiful one" to arouse her from a place of comfort.

What do these verses say to you?

_____
_____
_____
_____
_____
_____

These next verses from 2 Corinthians tell me if we are in a war and we have weapons, we must have an enemy!

"For though we live in the world, we do not wage war as the world does. The weapons we fight with are not the weapons of the world. On the contrary, they have divine power to demolish strongholds. We demolish arguments and every pretension that sets itself up against the knowledge of God, and we take captive every thought to make it obedient to Christ." (2 Cor. 10:3-5)

Spiritual warfare is taking back the territory and coming into agreement with the good report, we can do it! We take back the land given to us—for us and our future generations. What feels like an attack is actually enemy resistance because you entered the territory where he has his couch and refrigerator! It is the place he has made his home. We initiate the conflict to assert the dominion and authority of God.

Discipline and self-control aren't enough to change spiritual atmospheres. A good example is the person addicted to alcohol or food. They can stop excess consumption through will power, but the heart will still be hurting and the enemy will still occupy a stronghold. No one can "white knuckle" their way to inner freedom.

Freedom isn't something we do; it must be who we are. This hits precisely at the core of our enemies attack —the opposition against our identity in Him. It was the source of doubt used against Eve, it was the source of temptation against Jesus in the wilderness, and it was the source of fear that pricked Thomas' orphan heart.

The lies we believe fortify the enemies stronghold. In the enemy's game there is no love, no mercy, and no forgiveness. He is a liar and the father of lies (John 8:44).

Dancing on the Graves of Your Past Workbook

Look back over your answers from Chapter 2, ask Papa God if, because of what happened, were there any lies you believed.

#1 What happened?
_____
_____

#2 How I responded…
_____
_____
_____

#3 *"Papa God, because of what happened, are there any lies I believed?"*
_____
_____
_____
_____

#4 *"Papa God, do I still need to protect myself by believing this lie?"*_____

If *no*, pray, *"I ask you to forgive me for believing this lie and I come out of agreement and renounce the lie of* _____."
*"Papa, what is the truth?"*_____
_____
_____
_____

When you know the truth, the truth will set you free (John 8:32).

"Papa God, because of the lies, would You show me if there are there any vows, pledges, or promises I made to protect myself? Write what He shows you…

"Is it safe for me to renounce these vows, pledges, or promises now?"

_____
_____
_____

Now, come out of agreement with the vow, pledge, or promise.

"Papa God, I take full responsibility for my ungodly and unholy vow, pledge or promise and I ask You to forgive me for the vow, pledge, or promise of_____.

I renounce the vow pledge, or promise AND

through the power of Your Blood, I come out of agreement with the vow, pledge, or promise of_____.

I receive Your forgiveness and mercy.

Now that I have given this to You,

do You have something for me in exchange?"

_____
_____
_____
_____
_____
_____
_____
_____
_____
_____

_____
_____
_____
_____

How do you feel now?

_____
_____
_____
_____
_____

Next we will address the orphan spirit and allies.

Read John 14

Jesus discerned Thomas' insecurity and fear. In recognition of Thomas attitude, Jesus identifies an "orphan" spirit manifested in Thomas' fear of being left alone, unprotected, uncovered, rejected and abandoned.

The door to the orphan spirit is experienced when trauma breaks through the barriers of safety. Survival insists that something cover the gaping wound.

Now that you have forgiven, identified lies and broken soul ties, renounced vows, pledges and promises, it is time to get rid of the orphan spirit. It is time to renounce and come out of agreement with the lie that you have been left unprotected, uncovered, rejected and abandoned. The orphan spirit attacks identity by wanting you to believe you don't belong. However, the truth is that you do...

"For you did not receive a spirit that makes you a slave again to fear, but you have received the Spirit of sonship. And by him we cry, Abba Father. The Spirit himself testifies with our spirit that we are God's children." Romans 8:15,16

In what ways have you experienced an orphan spirit?

_____
_____
_____
_____
_____
_____
_____
_____

By coming out of agreement with the orphan spirit, you are allowing Papa God to claim you, to name you, to call you His own.

Are you ready to get rid of the orphan spirit? _____

If the answer is "yes," then pray...

"Papa God, I ask You to forgive me for agreeing with the orphan spirit. I renounce the orphan spirit that has lied to me that I am unprotected, uncovered, alone, abandoned, and have been left to find my own way. I come out of agreement with the lies of

_____

AND

I break* the power of the orphan spirit in the Name of Jesus."

"Papa, what is the truth?"

_____
_____
_____
_____
_____
_____
_____
_____
_____
_____
_____
_____
_____
_____
_____

"Papa, do YOU claim me?" _____

"Do YOU have a new name for me?" _____

If "yes," what is it?
_____

So, how are you doing with all this?
_____
_____
_____
_____

Are you ready to get rid of the unloving spirit? _____

If the answer is "yes," then pray…

"Papa God, I ask You to forgive me for agreeing with an unloving spirit and denying myself the full extent of Your love. I renounce the unloving spirit that has lied to me that I am unloveable or unacceptable. I break* the lie that the Cross and Jesus Blood wasn't full proof of God's love for me and I break* the lie that I can't trust and love others. I come out of agreement with the lies and I break* the power of the unloving spirit in the Name of Jesus."

"Papa, what is the truth?"

_____
_____
_____
_____
_____
_____
_____
_____
_____
_____

Are you ready to get rid of the religious spirit? _____

If the answer is "yes," then pray...

"Papa God, I ask You to forgive me for agreeing with a religious spirit and denying myself the full extend of Jesus' Cross and Blood. I renounce the religious spirit that has lied to me that I need to control or manipulate and "do" in order to "be." I come out of agreement with the fear of trusting others and You.

I break* the lie that the Cross and Jesus Blood isn't sufficient to protect me. I come out of agreement with the lies and I break* the power of the religious spirit in the Name of Jesus."

"Papa, what is the truth?"

_____
_____
_____
_____
_____
_____
_____
_____
_____
_____
_____
_____
_____

Are you ready to get rid of the punishing spirit? _____

If the answer is "yes," then pray...

"Papa God, I ask You to forgive me for agreeing with a punishing spirit and denying myself Your full payment for my sins through Jesus' Cross and Blood. I renounce the punishing spirit that has lied to me that I have to continue to punish myself for the things Jesus died to give me.

I ask You to forgive me for believing the lie that I don't deserve the benefits of the Kingdom or any way I have denied myself the blessings, gifts, and destiny You have given me through Jesus resurrection..

I break* the lie that the Cross and Jesus Blood isn't sufficient to pay for all my sin and wrong doing. I come out of agreement with the lies and I break* the power of the punishing spirit in the Name of Jesus."

"Papa, what is the truth?"

_____
_____
_____
_____
_____
_____
_____
_____
_____
_____
_____

Read John 14:17 and John 14:26

Do you want to experience the Holy Spirit? _____

If "yes," then pray...

"Papa God, I invite the Holy Spirit, the comforter and counselor, to fill me with His Presence. I come into agreement with the Spirit of Truth and receive the Truth of Your love, presence, and reality."

What is God showing you now?

_____
_____
_____
_____
_____
_____
_____
_____

Now, ask Papa to send you His Spirit of Adoption …

_____
_____

What is He showing you?

_____
_____
_____
_____
_____
_____
_____
_____
_____
_____
_____
_____

Handling future thoughts...

Thoughts that linger and persist consume our productivity, demanding our attention. They are usually thoughts that strike a vulnerable or unresolved emotional area and become a trigger point.

When the thought is persistent, you don't know the source or can't resolve it, challenge it with the following process.

Is this condemnation or conviction?

Condemnation is from the enemy. It produces false guilt with spiritual death as a goal. It overshadows and points to mistakes or sin. Condemnation's motive is an invitation to resurrect the gravesite of your past, returning to relationship with the Old Music and Old Dances.

Conviction is from the Holy Spirit. It produces true guilt with holiness as a goal. It overshadows and points to mistakes or sin. Conviction's motive invites you to surrender the situation to the gravesite and return your focus on the resurrected Christ in you uniting in relationship with Him.

Is this temptation or a test?

Temptation is from the enemy. Its goal is sin and separation from God. The attractive package contains handcuffs. If you indulge, the attraction will turn to distraction and condemnation will scream accusations.

A test is from God. Its goal is Christian character and draws us closer to God. Tests are often lessons in stewardship. They don't always feel good but ultimately work for our good.

If the thoughts are about sins, behaviors, attitudes OR from protectors or lies that were surrendered and prayed through, you've asked for forgiveness and you have forgiven others, then stand firm, rejecting the lie.

_____
_____
_____

If you are not sure, pray about it immediately. Resolve the guilt by accepting any of your personal responsibility.

Ask and receive God's forgiveness.

_____
_____
_____

If it is something you are not responsible for, then place responsibility where it belongs then surrender and forgive.

Resist and stand firm, rejecting the lie.

_____
_____
_____

Discerning the voice of the Good Shepherd is important. Jesus tells us that we will know His voice (John 10:14). Discernment protects you from receiving a false comforter or self-protective behavior which is a lie baited with pain, stress or fear, etc.

The voice of the Good Shepherd will always lead you. The voice of another will drive you. Refuse to follow the voice of "another." Allow the Spirit of Truth, who is in you, to keep your motives pure. Being tempted does not mean you are sinning. Remember, Jesus was tempted and refuted the lies with truth.

Learn your trigger points. What are the circumstances that cause you to lose your peace?

If you feel triggered, a key is to ask God to show you what He wants you to know about yourself and that situation. Then surrender, forgive and renounce any lies, receive His truth.

Revelation opens the door to access.

Read Matthew 14:35-36... what do these scriptures tell you?

_____
_____
_____
_____
_____

Chapter 8

Dance of the Kingdom

"Now unto him who is able to do immeasurably
more than all we ask or imagine…"
— Ephesians. 3:20

Read *Dancing on the Graves of Your Past*, Chapter 8~

God partnered with us in our past so we could partner with Him in our future. When you partner with God in the Dance of the Kingdom, you are fulfilling Paul's exhortation to leave our past behind and press on toward the higher calling in Jesus (Phil. 4:13,14). Partnering with God is taking our seat in Heavenly places with Christ Jesus (Eph. 2:6) with full access to our identity and inheritance in Jesus.

Are you ready to accept your seat in Heavenly places with Papa?
_____

Pray and ask Papa to show you what your seat look like?
_____
_____
_____
_____
_____

The Divine purpose of dancing in the Kingdom is to demonstrate His Presence by answering people's hearts and prophesying their destiny. God is actually interested in your desires and dreams. Paul called it "co-laboring" with Christ.

Read 2 Cor. 6:1

What are your desires and dreams?
_____
_____
_____
_____
_____

God is creative. He creates. It is who He is and what He does! He created man in His image and inherent in that image is the desire to create. When we create we are most like our Father. He created the original and we become imitators, illustrators of His nature, drawing attention to the true original.

In what way are you an imitator of Him?

_____
_____
_____
_____

Read Proverbs 8:22-35

What do these verses tell you about Wisdom being the creative Spirit of God?

_____
_____
_____
_____
_____
_____
_____
_____

Wisdom is the craftsman that creates inventions, technology, governmental institutions, administrations, social systems, engineering, architecture, science, medical breakthroughs, and so on.

How does Wisdom speak to you?

_____
_____
_____
_____
_____
_____
_____

We expand the territory of God by releasing what He has given us and demonstrating who we are called to be, His friends. Jesus said, "I no longer call you servants, because a servant does not know his master's business. Instead, I have called you friends, for everything that I learned from my Father I have made known to you" (John 15:15). We are God's friend. Friends talk, share, commune, laugh and cry together. They share dreams, ideas, and plan to spend time together. Friendship is greater than servanthood but it doesn't replace it. Friends are the greatest servants of all because they serve out of love not out of duty.

How do you demonstrate your friendship with Jesus?

_____
_____

As friends of God, our inheritance of wisdom and creativity is to be released to the world.

Ask Papa God right now... *"What ideas do You want to give me to transform business, governments, or nations?"*

Sometimes when we day dream or our mind wonders it is actually God taking us on a revelatory adventure. The co-laboring adventure may be for you or for someone else. It releases you into the prophetic—hearing from God for the people.

Do you hear from God on behalf of others? _____

What does that look like for you?

_____
_____
_____
_____

The Holy Spirit descended on the Lamb of God and remained giving Truth, Comfort and Counsel. Tenderness of heart yielded in "son-ship" unlocks Gods mysteries and revelation is ushered in by the Holy Spirit.

Ask Papa for a greater awareness of His Peace to you now...

_____
_____

Ask Papa to bring you the gift of Joy...

_____
_____

Chapter 9

Dance Face to Face

"Come! Whoever is thirsty, let him come; and whoever wishes, let him take the free gift of the water of life."
—Revelation 22:17

Read *Dancing on the Graves of Your Past*, Chapter 9 ~

Spiritual hunger can be satisfied by one thing—His Presence. The intimacy of God's presence fulfills all desire. Haggai 2:7 speaks prophetically of the "desire of all nations will come, and I will fill this house with glory."

Jesus fulfills the desire of man's longing. It isn't doing something for Him or Him doing something for you.

Read 2 Cor 3:18

It is being with Him without barriers. It is our "unveiled face" that reflects His glory.

Ask Papa to come now and reveal His Glory in your life...

_____
_____
_____
_____

Everything is to lead us into His embrace—the resting place of His Presence. The dance of a lifetime is the intimate Dance Face to Face. Being present with His Presence is a spiritual encounter with the King of Kings.

Many times our physical body is the scene of the crime committed against us. We can hold in our body the residual effects of trauma.

Ask Papa... "Do I have any physical issues connected with the trauma?"

_____
_____
_____
_____
_____
_____
_____
_____

If "yes", put your hand on that area of your body and pray this...

"Papa, I ask You to forgive me for any way, known or unknown, that I caused my body to suffer for the emotional pain I have experienced."

With your hand on that area of your body, speak to your body...

"Body, I ask you to forgive me for making you perform past your limits. I ask you to forgive me for stressing you with bad habits. I ask you to forgive me for punishing you, hurting you or making you endure hardship."

"I come out of agreement with a spirit of trauma now in Jesus Name. I break the spirit of trauma off my spirit, mind and my body. I come out of agreement with infirmity and break* it off my spirit mind and body now."*

Try doing something you couldn't do before. For example, if your knee was stiff, try moving it...

What is happening now?

_____
_____
_____
_____
_____

Kingdom power is inside of you in the form of the Holy Spirit as Jesus told us in Luke 17:21 "For behold, the kingdom of God is within you."

Read John 14:17

What is God telling you about this verse?

_____
_____
_____
_____
_____

The Holy Spirit is both around us and in us signifying His presence both external and internal.

The external Kingdom is experienced when we enter into an atmosphere of worship or sit under the anointing of a leader and we are affected by the Presence of God around us. "Soaking" was the term used to describe lying down quietly and allowing the external atmospheric Presence of God to penetrate into our spirit.

When we learn to experience the internal Kingdom we access the "living water" Jesus gives so we will never be thirsty again. The unending source of the Kingdom inside us goes with us wherever we go. When He lifts the curtain of our senses to perceive Him, we have entered the Dance, Face to Face.

This is an exercise to access the internal Kingdom of God.

Read Psalm 16

Pick a verse you like. Which one did you pick? _____

Ok, now you are going to use that verse to access the Kingdom.

This is not an empting of your mind like some new age ritual...this is using your mind to access Him. We actually make our mind focus on what our spirit is connecting with, rather than letting our mind run around like a 2 yr old causing chaos everywhere it ventures!

So you begin to focus on the scripture and press in...meaning you stay focused and concentrated on the verse...this allows the Holy Spirit to meet you and bring you into the Kingdom...accessing Heaven in YOU!

If your mind wanders, bring it back into focus with the scripture, repeat the scripture and force your mind to stay at task by letting your spirit be in charge. Keep doing this until your spirit can stay focused on the connection with the Kingdom. He will lead you into an encounter with His Presence IN YOU!

What is happening when you experience the connection with His Kingdom in you?

_____
_____
_____

"Then Mary took about a pint of pure nard, an expensive perfume; she poured it on Jesus' feet and wiped his feet with her hair. And the house was filled with the fragrance of the perfume" (John 12:3). It is most likely as Mary poured out the perfume it dripped or splashed on her hands, arms and clothing which probably offended the crowd even more! She didn't let the taunts and criticism stop her from pouring and smearing the perfume on Jesus allowing whatever overflow to inadvertently drip onto her. Interestingly, the word "Christ" means *anointed one* and is actually translated *"to smear."* When we press in and step pass the religious spirit, we, too will be smeared with the anointing of the Holy Spirit. And the fragrant scent of His Presence will be a sign we have been with Him.

So, my friend, put flowers on the graves of your past and say "goodbye." The world is your stage. Let the curtain of heaven open. He has arrived. Dance with Him. Dance on the graves of your past. Dance in His Kingdom, dance in His arms, dance while gazing into His face. Dance tenderly, dance in joy, dance wildly, dance with happy feet. Dance like no one is looking then dance for the world to see.

He is here... "May I have this dance?"

Go ahead, dance with Him! Write your experience...

_____
_____
_____
_____
_____

"…as the movement grew yet swifter, the interweaving yet more ecstatic, the relevance of all to all yet more intense, as dimension was added to dimension and that part of him which could reason and remember was dropped farther and farther behind that part of him which saw, even then, at the very zenith of complexity, complexity was eaten up and faded, as a thin white cloud fades into the hard blue burning of the sky, and a simplicity beyond all comprehension, ancient and young as spring, illimitable, pellucid, drew him with cords of infinite desire into its own stillness. He went up into such a quietness, a privacy, and a freshness that at the very moment when he stood farthest from our ordinary mode of being he had the sense of stripping off encumbrances and awaking from trance, and coming to himself."

C.S. Lewis, Perelandra, excerpt from pp. 218-219

About the Author

Yvonne is the author of 5 books, conference speaker, third-year Bethel School of Supernatural Ministry graduate, and hosts articles and Q/A column for the Christian Quarterly entitled *Talk With Yvonne*.

With 25 years experience in prophetic counseling and pastoring, emotional healing and trauma resolution, Yvonne serves on Pastoral Counseling staff in the Transformation Center at Bethel Church in Redding, CA. She also ministers with the Bethel Sozo team and is part of their mentoring program.

As an ordained minister, Yvonne's passion is to see people acquire their Kingdom identity, inheritance, intimacy and authority. She is available for speaking or personal ministry.

CONTACT

Yvonne Martinez

(530) 255-2099 x 1921

yvonnem@ibethel.org or talkwithyvonne@hotmail.com

Book and workbook available at

www.StillwaterLavender.com

Bethel Church website: www.ibethel.org

Bethel Sozo website: www.bethelsozo.com

If you have a testimony from the workbook you would like to share, Yvonne would love to hear from you.

Made in the USA
Lexington, KY
28 April 2012